SNOWBOARDING BLAST

SNOWBOARD HALF-PIPE

by Cara Krenn

CAPSTONE PRESS
a capstone imprint

Published by Capstone Press, an imprint of Capstone
1710 Roe Crest Drive, North Mankato, Minnesota 56003
capstonepub.com

Library of Congress Cataloging-in-Publication Data is available on the Library of Congress website.
ISBN: 9798875255885 (hardcover)
ISBN: 9798875255830 (paperback)
ISBN: 9798875255847 (ebook PDF)

Summary: Snowboard half-pipe riders never stop pushing the limits with their stunning midair tricks. Learn about the most amazing snowboard half-pipe tricks, how they are scored, and who the superstars are in this thrilling sport.

Editorial Credits
Editor: Carrie Sheely; Designer: Hilary Wacholz; Media Researcher: Rebekah Hubstenberger; Production Specialist: Tori Abraham

Image Credits
Alamy: Taka Wu, 21; Associated Press: Chris Dillmann/Vail Daily, 6; Getty Images: Al Bello, 20, Cameron Spencer, 24, 25, Cavan Images/Ben Girardi, cover, Doug Pensinger, 19, 22-23, Ezra Shaw, 16-17, 18, 29, iStock/So-CoAddict, 10-11, Jamie Squire, 4-5, 13, Maja Hitij, 27, Matthew Stockman, 12, Matthias Hangst, 8-9, 26, Nathan Bilow/Agence Zoom, 28; Newscom: Kyodo, 14-15

Design Elements
Shutterstock: AlexanderTrou, kostins, Rosovskyi, SAI A.D.A, sergio34

Printed and bound in China. 006459

TABLE OF CONTENTS

Words in **bold** are in the glossary.

CHAPTER 1

DROPPING IN

A snowboarder stands at the top of the half-pipe. *Whoosh!* She drops in and gains speed. The excited crowd watches closely. She flies into the air.

SALOMON

What amazing trick will she do? The double crippler! She does two backflips. Now it's on to the next daring trick.

Double crippler

LET'S TALK SNOWBOARD HALF-PIPE!

air: being above the half-pipe

cork: the combination of a rotation the rider does at an angle and a flip; the trick looks like a corkscrew

flip: a somersault in the air

grab: to hold on to the edge of a snowboard during a trick

half-pipe: a U-shaped ramp with high sides

rotation: a spin of the body in the air

run: a ride down the half-pipe in which a rider performs tricks

CHAPTER 2

BIG AIR!

In half-pipe, snowboarders ride high into the air. How high? Some go higher than a two-story building from the half-pipe's top! Riders perform flips, spins, grabs, and other tricks.

LAUSANNE 2020
LAUSANNE 2020

HALF-PIPE FEATURES

deck
transition

What do half-pipe riders need to compete? First, they need to be fearless! They also need great **balance**. They practice a lot to improve their skills.

Riders learn to control their bodies in the air. As they come down, they stay focused on their landing spot. One small mistake could cause a fall.

Double cork 1260

As riders gain skill, they move on to harder tricks. Top riders do tricks such as the double cork 1260. It has two **diagonal** flips and three and a half **rotations**.

CHAPTER 3

COMPETITION TIME

The top competitions are the Winter Olympics and the Winter X Games. Large crowds gather to watch these exciting events. The Olympics happen every four years. The X Games are every year.

FACT

Snowboard half-pipe became an Olympic sport in 1998.

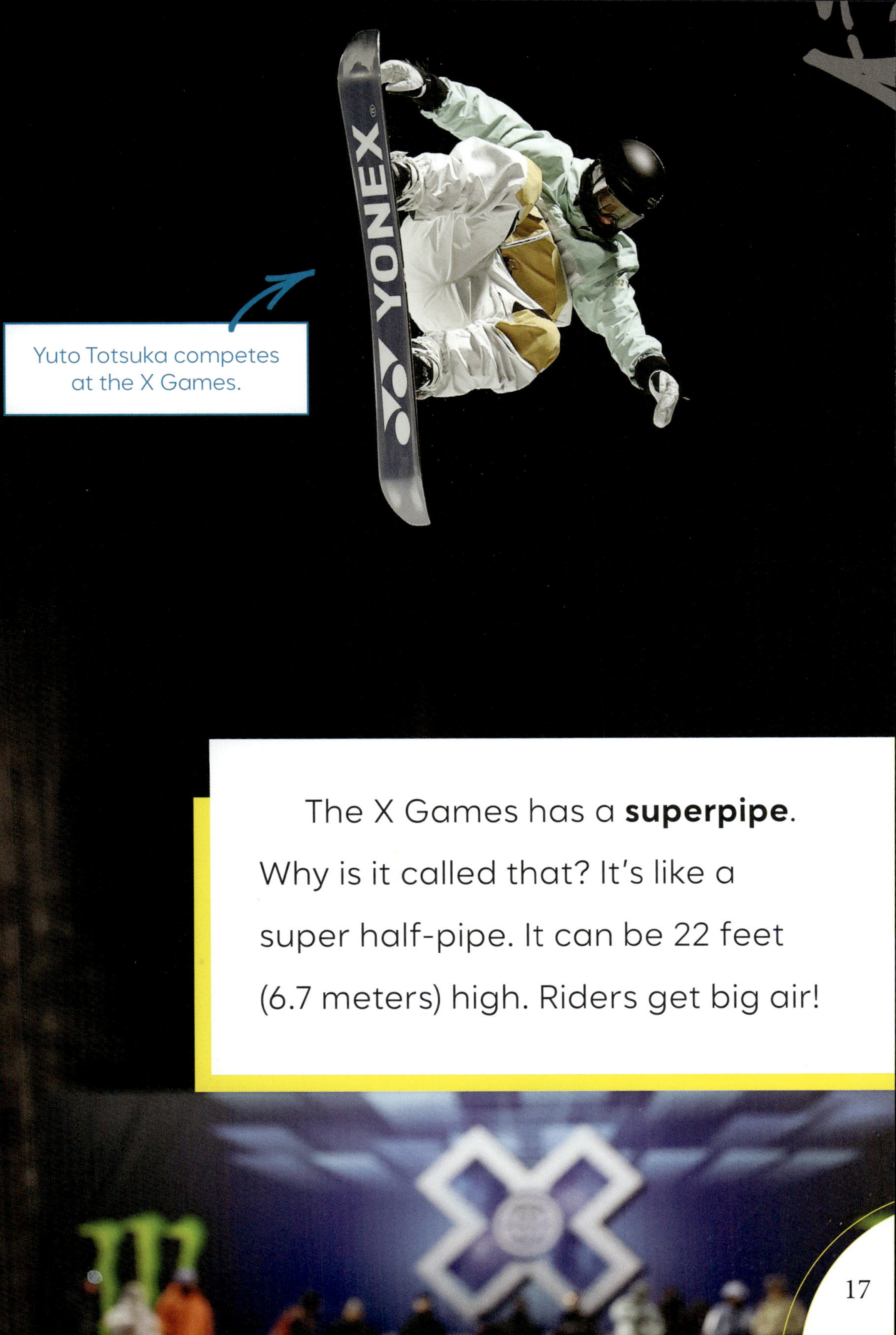

Yuto Totsuka competes at the X Games.

The X Games has a **superpipe**. Why is it called that? It's like a super half-pipe. It can be 22 feet (6.7 meters) high. Riders get big air!

Spin and flip! Riders show off their best tricks. They all want the top score! A run is scored from one to 100. One hundred is a perfect score. Has anyone ever gotten a perfect score? Yes! Shaun White and Chloe Kim did.

Shaun White performs the run that earned him a perfect 100 points at the 2012 X Games.

Riders get a certain number of **runs** in competitions. There is no time limit to finish a run.

Riders are judged on many things. How much height do they get in the air? How hard are their tricks? How many different tricks can they do? Judges also score riders on style and how they put tricks together.

FACT

Riders try to invent new tricks to impress both event judges and fans!

CHAPTER 4

HALF-PIPE HEROES

Shaun White is a snowboarding **legend**. He won three Olympic gold medals for the U.S. His nickname is the "Flying Tomato" because of his red hair. He has the record for the most X Games SuperPipe gold medals with eight.

White with his SuperPipe gold medal at the 2013 X Games

Kim competing in the final at the 2018 Olympics

Chloe Kim won her first X Games gold medal in SuperPipe when she was just 14. At 17, she won an Olympic gold medal. She was the first woman to complete back-to-back 1080s in competition.

Kim after winning a gold medal at the 2022 Olympics

Ayumu Hirano won a gold and two silver Olympic medals for Japan. He was the first to land the triple cork 1440 trick while competing.

Hirano competing at the 2022 Olympics

Ayumu Hirano with his gold medal at the 2022 Olympics

FACT

Hirano has competed in the Summer Olympics in skateboarding.

Kelly Clark in action at the 2015 X Games

Kelly Clark won a gold and two bronze medals for the U.S. She competed in more Winter X Games than any other athlete.

Scotty James won two Olympic medals for Australia. He won a gold medal at the Winter X Games six times.

Snowboard half-pipe is full of daring skills. Who will be the next top rider?

Scotty James competing at the 2025 X Games

GLOSSARY

balance (BAL-uhns)—to keep steady and not fall over

diagonal (dy-AY-guh-nuhl)—going in a slanted direction

legend (LEJ-uhnd)—someone who is among the best in what they do

rotation (roh-TAY-shuhn)—a spin of the body

run (RUN)—a ride down the half-pipe in which a rider performs tricks

superpipe (SOO-pur-pipe)—a very big half-pipe with steep walls; the X Games superpipe that riders compete on is called a SuperPipe

READ MORE

Goldstein, Margaret J. *Meet Chloe Kim.* Minneapolis: Lerner Publications, 2023.

Herman, Gail. *What Are the Winter Olympics?* New York: Penguin Workshop, 2021.

Pryor, Shawn. *Who Is Shaun White?* New York: Penguin Workshop, 2024.

INTERNET SITES

Everything You Need to Know About Halfpipe Skiing and Snowboarding
redbull.com/us-en/half-pipe-ski-snowboard-guide

Olympic Games: Chloe Kim
olympics.com/en/athletes/chloe-kim

Olympic Games: Shaun White
olympics.com/en/athletes/shaun-white

INDEX

ABOUT THE AUTHOR

Cara Krenn writes children's books and for a variety of kids' magazines on topics ranging from trash trucks to magical creatures. She thinks a well-chosen book makes the perfect gift. Cara loves the beach, dance music, and morning walks with her cowardly dog. She is a graduate of the University of Notre Dame and lives in sunny San Diego with her husband, twin daughters, and son.